Table of contents

It's helpful to plan ahead, consider all your long-term care options, and make good financial plans early.

Section 1:
Getting started

People go to nursing homes for different reasons, including if they're sick, hurt, had surgery and need to get better, or have chronic care needs or disabilities that require on-going nursing care. "Your Guide to Choosing a Nursing Home or Other Long-Term Care" can help you make informed decisions about nursing home care, whether you're planning ahead or need to make an unexpected decision.

Before you get started

You may have other long-term care choices, like community services, home care, or assisted living, depending on your needs and resources. Before choosing a nursing home, you can check to see if one of these other options is available to you or if they might help after a nursing home stay. For more information on your long-term care choices, see Section 3.

If you have Medicare

Medicare generally doesn't cover long-term care stays in a nursing home. See Section 5 for more information.

If you have Medicaid

You may be eligible for home- and community-based services covered by Medicaid. You may also be eligible for in-home, long-term supports and services if you have a disability, regardless of your age. See Section 5 for more information.

Not all nursing homes are certified to participate in Medicare or Medicaid. See pages 47–52 for more information on how programs protect nursing home residents.

When you're in a nursing home, it's important to get preventive care, like a yearly flu shot, to help you stay healthy.

Section 2:
Where to get help

Administration for Community Living (ACL)

The ACL is a part of the federal government that supports services to help you with information and assistance regarding long-term supports and services in your community:

Eldercare Locator

The Eldercare Locator is a public service to help older adults and their caregivers connect to services, including long-term care services and supports.

eldercare.gov

1-800-677-1116

Aging and Disability Resource Centers (ADRCs)

ACL partners with the Centers for Medicare & Medicaid Services (CMS), the Veterans Health Administration, and other federal agencies to support state's development of "No Wrong Door Systems" that streamline access to long-term services and supports. States are at different stages of developing their "No Wrong Door Systems." ADRCs are part of "No Wrong Door Systems."

All 50 states and 4 territories (District of Columbia, Guam, Puerto Rico, and the Commonwealth of the Northern Mariana Islands) currently have or will soon have an ADRC. Older adults, people with disabilities, caregivers, and families can use ADRCs to enter the long-term services and supports system. ADRCs help individuals and their families identify their long-term services and support needs, understand their options including the publicly funded programs available to them, and develop and activate a long-term care plan.

Use the Eldercare Locator at 1-800-677-1116, or visit adrc-tae.gov for information about services available in your area.

Long-Term Care Ombudsman

Long-Term Care Ombudsman are advocates for residents of nursing homes, board and care homes, assisted living facilities, and similar adult care facilities. They work to resolve problems of individual residents and to bring about changes at the local, state, and national levels that will improve residents' care and quality of life.

Long-Term Care Ombudsman:

- Visit nursing homes and speak with residents throughout the year to make sure residents' rights are protected
- Work to solve problems with your nursing home care, including financial issues
- Discuss general information about nursing homes and nursing home care
- Help you compare a nursing home's strengths and weaknesses
- Answer questions, like how many complaints they've gotten about a specific nursing home, what kind of complaints they were, and if the issues were resolved in a timely manner

ACL supports the National Ombudsman Resource Center, which has contact information for States' Long-Term Care Ombudsman Programs:

ltcombudsman.org

Use the Eldercare Locator at 1-800-677-1116 to get the phone number for your local ombudsman program office.

Centers for Independent Living (CILs)

Centers for Independent Living (CILs) support people with disabilities find community living options and develop independent living skills.

Visit www.ilru.org/hmlt/publications/directory/index.html for contact information of local services.

Words in blue are defined on pages 53–54.

Centers for Medicare & Medicaid Services (CMS)

CMS is an agency in the federal government that can give you more information about Medicare and Medicaid coverage, home and community-based services, and other health-related topics.

Medicare.gov

1-800-MEDICARE (1-800-633-4227)

TTY: 1-877-486-2048

Nursing Home Compare

Medicare's Nursing Home Compare allows you to find and compare information about nursing homes. See page 18 for more information.

Medicare.gov/nhcompare

Quality Improvement Organizations (QIOs)

Your QIO can help if you have questions or want to report complaints about the quality of your care for a Medicare-covered service or if you think Medicare coverage for your service is ending too soon. A QIO is a group of practicing doctors and other health care experts paid by the federal government to check and improve the care given to people with Medicare.

Visit Medicare.gov/contacts, or call 1-800-MEDICARE (1-800-633-4227) to get the phone number for the QIO in your state. TTY users should call 1-877-486-2048.

State Health Insurance Assistance Programs (SHIPs)

Your SHIP can give you free health insurance counseling. SHIPs are state programs that get money from the federal government to give free, local health insurance counseling.

Visit Medicare.gov/contacts, or call 1-800-MEDICARE to get the phone number for the SHIP in your state.

State Medical Assistance (Medicaid) offices

Medicaid offices are state agencies that are in charge of the state's Medicaid Program. Your state Medicaid office can give you information about Medicaid eligibility and covered benefits, including coverage for institutional (nursing home) and home- and community-based long-term care services.

Visit Medicare.gov/contacts, or call 1-800-MEDICARE to get the phone number for your state Medicaid office.

Medicaid.gov

State Survey Agencies

Your State Survey Agency can help with questions or complaints about the quality of care or the quality of life in a nursing home. State Survey Agencies are state agencies that oversee nursing homes that participate in the Medicare and/or Medicaid programs. State Survey Agencies inspect health care facilities and investigate complaints to ensure health and safety standards are met.

Call 1-800-MEDICARE (1-800-633-4227) to get the phone number for your State Survey Agency. TTY users should call 1-877-486-2048.

Section 3:

Choosing the type of care you need

Depending on your needs and resources, you may have other long-term care options (besides nursing home care) available to you. For example, you may be able to get the services and supports you need in your own home or in other types of community housing. If you're in a hospital, nursing home, or working with a home health agency (HHA), talk to: a discharge planner, a social worker, an organization in a "No Wrong Door System," like an Aging and Disability Resource Center (ADRC), Area Agency on Aging, or Center for Independent Living (CIL) to understand your options or help you arrange care.

Each state and community has different services and options available. Contact your state's "No Wrong Door System" through their website, phone number, or local community organization, like an ARDC, Area Agency on Aging, Intellectual and Developmental Disability organization, or CIL for more information. See page 7. American Indians and Alaska Natives can contact their local Indian health care providers for more information.

Alternative long-term care choices

Below are some common types of long-term services and supports. Talk to your family, your doctor or other health care provider, a person-centered counselor, or a social worker for help deciding what kind of long-term care you need. In many states, ADRCs provide person-centered counseling to help you understand, evaluate, and manage the full range of services and supports available in your community. ADRCs provide "options counseling" to help you understand, evaluate, and manage the full range of services and supports available in your community. See page 7.

Note: If you have limited income and resources, there may be state programs that help cover some of your costs in some of the long-term care choices mentioned below. Call your State Medical Assistance (Medicaid) office, the Eldercare Locator, or an ADRC for more information. See page 7.

Choosing the type of care you need

Words in blue are defined on pages 53–54.

Community services: A variety of community services may help with your personal care and activities, as well as home modification and equipment to support you staying at home. Some services, like volunteer groups that help with things like shopping or transportation, may be low cost or may ask for a voluntary donation. Some services may be available at varied costs depending on where you live and the services you need. These home services and programs may be available in your community:

- Adult day care
- Adult day health care, which offers nursing and therapy
- Meal programs
- Senior centers
- Friendly visitor programs
- Help with shopping and transportation
- Help with legal questions, bill pay, and other financial matters

For information about community services, use the Eldercare Locator or an ADRC. See page 7.

Home care: Depending on your needs, you may be able to get help with your personal care and activities (like laundry, shopping, cooking, and cleaning) at home from family members, friends, or volunteer groups. Home care agencies are also available to help with personal care, like bathing and help walking.

If you think you need home care, talk to your family to see if they can help with your care or help arrange for other care providers. There are also some home health care agencies that can help with nursing or attendant care in your home. If you're eligible for Medicaid, personal care and other long-term care services and supports in your home may be covered.

Home health care: There are also some home health care agencies that can help with nursing care in your home. Home health care agencies may also provide other services, like physical therapy, occupational therapy, and help bathing.

Medicare only covers short-term home health care if you meet certain limited conditions. For more information on Medicare's coverage of home health care, visit Medicare.gov.

Accessory dwelling units (ADUs): If you or a loved one owns a single-family home, adding an ADU to an existing home may help you keep your independence. An ADU (sometimes called an "in-law apartment," "accessory apartment," "or a "second unit") is a second living space within a home or on a lot. It has a separate living and sleeping area, a place to cook, and a bathroom. Space like an upper floor, basement, attic, or over a garage may be turned into an ADU. Family members may be interested in living in an ADU in your home, or you may want to build a separate living space at a family member's home.

Check with your local zoning office to be sure ADUs are allowed in your area and find out if there are special rules. The cost for an ADU can vary widely depending on the size and cost of building materials and workers.

Subsidized senior housing: There are state and federal programs that help pay for housing for some older people with low to moderate incomes. Some of these housing programs also offer help with meals and other activities, like housekeeping, shopping, and doing the laundry. Residents usually live in their own apartments within an apartment building. Rent payments are usually a percentage of your income.

Residential care facilities (board and care homes, and assisted living): Board and care homes (sometimes called "group homes" or "personal care homes") and assisted living communities are group living arrangements. In some states, board and care homes and assisted living mean the same thing. Board and care homes and assisted living communities provide help with some of the activities of daily living, like bathing, dressing, and using the bathroom. Whether they provide nursing services or help with medications varies among states.

Choosing the type of care you need

In assisted living, residents often live in their own room or apartment within a building or group of buildings and have some or all of their meals together. Social and recreational activities are usually provided. Some of these facilities have health services on site.

In most cases, board and care home, and assisted living residents pay a regular monthly rent and pay additional fees for the services they get. Medicare doesn't pay for assisted living facilities. Medicaid doesn't pay for room and board in these settings, but, depending on the state, may cover long-term services and support costs. The term "assisted living" may mean different things in different facilities within the same state. Not all assisted living facilities provide the same services. It's important to contact the facility and to make sure they can meet your needs.

The Long-Term Care Ombudsman can help people who live in these types of settings. See page 7.

Continuing Care Retirement Communities (CCRCs): CCRCs are retirement communities that offer more than one kind of housing and different levels of care. In the same community, there may be individual homes or apartments for residents who still live on their own, an assisted living facility for people who need some help with daily care, and a nursing home for those who require higher levels of care.

Residents move from one level to another based on their individual needs, but usually stay within the CCRC. If you're considering a CCRC, be sure to check the quality information (see pages 18–24) and inspection report (posted in the facility) of its nursing home. Your CCRC contract usually requires you to use the CCRC's nursing home if you need nursing home care. Some CCRCs will only admit people into their nursing home who are already living in another section of the retirement community.

CCRCs generally require a large payment before you move in (called an "entry fee") and charge monthly fees.

Hospice care: Hospice is a program of care and support for people who are terminally ill. The focus is on comfort, not on curing an illness.

If you qualify for hospice care and choose to get the hospice benefit, hospice services may include physical care, counseling, drugs, equipment, and supplies for the terminal illness and related condition(s). As part of hospice care, you'll have a specially trained team of professionals and caregivers to provide care, including taking care of your physical, emotional, social, and spiritual needs.

The hospice benefit allows you and your family to stay together in the comfort of your home unless you need care in an inpatient facility. Some long-term care facilities and nursing homes offer hospice services from outside providers. If the hospice team determines that you need inpatient care, the hospice team will make the arrangements for your stay. Many nursing homes and residential care facilities also have contracts with hospice providers.

Medicare covers hospice care if you qualify. Medicare doesn't cover room and board if you get general hospice services while you're a resident of a nursing home or a hospice's residential facility. If you're eligible, Medicaid may pay for some services that Medicare doesn't cover, like personal care assistance at home. Medicare doesn't pay for 24-hour assistance if you get hospice services at home.

For more information on Medicare's coverage of hospice care and who qualifies, visit Medicare.gov.

Choosing the type of care you need

Respite care: Some nursing homes, residential care facilities, and hospice care facilities provide respite care. You may also get respite care in your home. Respite care is short-term assistance so the primary caregiver can rest. Medicare covers inpatient respite care for up to 5 days if you're getting covered hospice care services. Room and board are covered for inpatient respite care and during short-term hospital stays. If you're eligible, Medicaid will pay for some of these services at home that aren't covered by Medicare.

For more information on Medicare's coverage of respite care and who qualifies, visit Medicare.gov.

Programs of All-inclusive Care for the Elderly (PACE): PACE is a Medicare and Medicaid program offered in many states that allows people who otherwise need a nursing home-level of care to remain in the community.

To qualify for PACE, you must meet these conditions:

- You're 55 or older.
- You live in the service area of a PACE organization.
- You're certified by your state as needing a nursing home-level of care.
- At the time you join, you're able to live safely in the community with the help of PACE services.

To find out if you're eligible and if there's a PACE site near you, visit pace4you.org or Medicaid.gov, or you can call your State Medical Assistance (Medicaid) office. See page 38.

Home and community-based waiver programs: If you're already eligible for Medicaid (or, in some states, would be specifically eligible for Medicaid coverage for nursing home services), you may be able to get help with the costs of some home and community-based services, like homemaker services, personal care, and respite care. States have home and community-based waiver programs to help people keep their independence while getting the care they need outside of an inpatient facility.

For more information, visit Medicare.gov, or use the Eldercare Locator or an ADRC. See page 7.

Steps to choosing a nursing home

Follow these steps to find the nursing home that meets your needs.

Step 1: Find nursing homes in your area. See below.

Step 2: Compare the quality of the nursing homes you're considering. See page 18.

Step 3: Visit the nursing homes you're interested in or have someone visit for you. See pages 19–32.

Step 4: Choose the nursing home that meets your needs. See pages 33–36.

Step 1: Find nursing homes in your area.

To learn about the nursing homes in your area:

- Ask people you trust, like your family, friends, or neighbors if they've had personal experience with nursing homes. They may be able to recommend a nursing home to you.

- Ask your doctor if he or she provides care at any local nursing homes. If so, ask your doctor which nursing homes he or she visits so you may continue to see him or her while you're in the nursing home.

- Visit Medicare.gov/nhcompare to find nursing homes in your area.

- Use the Eldercare Locator or an ADRC. See page 7.

- Contact your local senior and community activity center.

- If you're in the hospital, ask your social worker about discharge planning as early in your hospital stay as possible. The hospital's staff should be able to help you find a nursing home that meets your needs and help with your transfer when you're ready to be discharged.

Step 2: Compare the quality of the nursing homes you're considering.

Medicare's Nursing Home Compare

Compare the care that nursing homes provide to help find the nursing home that meets your needs. Visit Medicare.gov/nhcompare to compare the nursing home quality of every Medicare and Medicaid-certified nursing home in the country.

Consider the information on Nursing Home Compare carefully. Use it along with other information you gather about nursing homes.

Note: Information on Nursing Home Compare isn't an endorsement or advertisement for any particular nursing home.

Other ways to find out about nursing home quality

You may want to use a variety of resources when choosing a nursing home:

- Visit the nursing homes you're considering, if possible, or have someone visit for you.
- Call your Long-Term Care Ombudsman. See page 7.
- Call your state health department or state licensing agency (look in the blue pages in the phone book or on the internet). Ask if they have written information on the quality of care given in local nursing homes. You can also ask for a copy of the full survey or the last complaint investigation report.
- Look at survey findings (CMS Form 2567) for the facility. They can be found on Nursing Home Compare or at each nursing home, typically in the lobby area.

Step 3: Visit the nursing homes you're interested in or have someone visit for you.

Before you visit any nursing homes, consider what's important to you and think about the questions below. Some of these questions ask about rights and protections that are guaranteed to you as a nursing home resident, like being treated in a respectful way. See pages 47–52 for more information on your guaranteed rights and protections. Other questions ask about preferences that may not be guaranteed, like bringing a pet into a nursing home. Be sure to think about what's important to you before you pick a nursing home.

Quality of life

- Will I be treated in a respectful way?
- How will the nursing home help me participate in social, recreational, religious, or cultural activities that are important to me? Can I decide when I want to participate?
- Do I get to choose what time to get up, go to sleep, or bathe?
- Can I have visitors at any time? Will the nursing home let me see visitors who may come to visit at early or late hours?
- Is transportation provided to community activities?
- Can I bring my pet or can my pet visit?
- Can I decorate my living space any way I want?
- How will the nursing home make sure I have privacy when I have visitors or personal care services?
- Would I be able to leave the facility for a few hours or days if I choose to do so? Are there procedures for leaving?

Steps to choosing a nursing home

Quality of care

- What's a plan of care and what does it look like?
- Who makes the plan of care and how do they know what I want, need, or what should be in the plan?
- Will I be included in planning my care?
    —Will my interests and preferences be included in the care plan?
    —Will I be able to change the plan if I feel there's a need?
    —Will I be able to choose which of my family members or friends will be involved in the planning process?
    —Will I get a copy of my care plan?
- Who are the doctors who will care for me? Can I still see my personal doctors? Who will help me arrange transportation if I choose to continue to see my personal doctors and they don't visit the nursing home?
- Who will give me the care I need?
- If a resident has a problem with confusion and wanders, how does the staff handle this type of behavior to protect the residents?
- Does the nursing home's inspection report show quality of care problems (deficiencies)?
- What does the quality information on Nursing Home Compare at Medicare.gov/nhcompare show about how well this nursing home cares for its residents?

Location

- Is the nursing home close to my family and friends so they can visit often?

Availability

- Is a bed available now or can I add my name to a waiting list?

    Note: Nursing homes don't have to accept all applications, but they must comply with local, state, and federal civil rights laws that prohibit discrimination.

Staffing

- Is there enough staff to give me the care I need?

- Will I have the same staff people take care of me day to day or do they change?

- Does the nursing home post information about the number of nursing staff, including Certified Nursing Assistants (CNAs)? Are they willing to show me if I ask to see it? (**Note:** Nursing homes are required to post this information.)

- How many residents is a CNA assigned to work with during each shift (day and night) and during meals?

- What type of therapy is available at this facility? Are therapy staff available?

- Is there a social worker available? Can I meet him or her? (**Note:** Nursing homes must provide medically related social services, but if the nursing home has less than 120 beds, it doesn't have to have a full-time social worker on staff.)

Religious & cultural preference

- Does the nursing home offer the religious or cultural support I need? If no, what type of arrangements will they provide to meet my needs?

- Do they provide special diet options that my faith practice may require?

Food & dining

- Does the nursing home have food service that I would be happy with?

- Does the nursing home provide a pleasant dining experience?

- Does the staff help residents eat and drink at mealtimes if help is needed?

- What types of meals does the nursing home serve? (**Note:** Ask the nursing home if you can see a menu.)

- Can I get food and drinks I like at any time? What if I don't like the food that's served?

- Do residents have a choice of food items at each meal? Are there options and substitutes available if I don't like a particular meal?

- Can the nursing home provide for my dietary needs?

Steps to choosing a nursing home

Language
- Is my primary language spoken by staff that will work directly with me and fellow residents?
- If not, is an interpreter available or another system in place to help me communicate my needs?

Policies
- Are there resident policies I must follow?
- Will I get a written copy of these policies?

  Note: Resident policies are rules that all residents must follow. For example, smoking may not be allowed in or on the premises of some nursing homes.

Security
- Does the nursing home provide a safe environment?
- Will my personal belongings be secure in my room?
- Is the nursing home locked at night?

Preventive care
- Does the nursing home make sure residents get preventive care to help keep them healthy? Are specialists like eye doctors, ear doctors, dentists, and podiatrists (foot doctors), available to see residents on a regular basis? Does the facility help make arrangements to see these specialists? (**Note:** Nursing homes must either provide treatment, or help you make appointments and provide transportation for you to see specialists.)
- Does the nursing home have a screening program for vaccinations, like flu (influenza) and pneumonia? (**Note:** Nursing homes are required to provide flu shots each year, but you have the right to refuse if you don't want the shot, have already been immunized during the immunization period, or if the shots are medically contraindicated.)
- How does the nursing home allow me access to oral care?
- How does the nursing home allow me access to mental health care?

Hospitals

- Does the nursing home have an arrangement with a nearby hospital for emergencies?
- Can my doctor care for me at that hospital?

Licensing

- Are the nursing home and current administrator licensed in my state?

Note: This means nursing homes have met certain standards set by a state or local government agency.

Certification (certified)

- Is the nursing home Medicare and/or Medicaid-certified?

Note: "Certified" means the nursing home meets Medicare and/or Medicaid regulations and the nursing home has passed and continues to pass an inspection survey done by the State Survey Agency. If they're certified, make sure they haven't recently lost their certification or are about to lose their certification. Also, some nursing homes may only have a certain "distinct part" of their building certified for Medicare or Medicaid residents.

Services

- What services does the nursing home provide? Does the nursing home have the services I need?

Charges & fees

- Will the nursing home tell me in writing about their services, charges, and fees before I move into the home?

Note: Medicare and/or Medicaid certified nursing homes must tell you this information in writing. Get a copy of the fee schedule to find out which services are available, which are included in your monthly fee, and which services cost extra? Then, compare nursing home costs.

- Is there a basic fee for room, meals, and personal care?
- Are there extra charges for other services, like beauty shop services?

Health & fire safety inspection reports

- Does the nursing home have the most recent health and fire inspection reports for me to look at?

  Note: Ask the staff to provide these reports. They tell you how well the nursing home meets federal health and safety regulations. The nursing home must have the report of the most recent state or federal survey of the facility available for you to look at. Reports can also be found on most State agency websites, as well as on Medicare.gov/nhcompare.

Resident, family, & satisfaction

- Can I talk to staff, residents, and family members of residents? Will I be able to ask them if they're satisfied with the nursing home and its services?

  Note: Any resident or family member of a resident has the right to refuse to talk to you. However, staff should be able to visit with you if they're not involved in care or service duties at the time. Also, many facilities have staff, resident, and family satisfaction surveys. You may want to ask to see the most recent survey results.

Visit the nursing homes

After you consider what's important to you in a nursing home, visit the nursing homes. It's best to visit the nursing homes that interest you before you make a final decision on which one meets your needs.

A visit gives you the chance to see the residents, staff, and the nursing home setting. It also allows you to ask questions of the nursing home staff and talk with residents and their family members.

If you can't visit the nursing home yourself, you may want to get a family member or friend to visit for you. If a family member or friend can't visit for you, you can call for information. However, a visit can help you see the quality of care and life of the actual residents.

Important things to know when visiting nursing homes

- Before you go, call and make an appointment to meet with someone on staff. You're also encouraged to visit the nursing homes at other times without an appointment. If a nursing home doesn't offer a "drop-in" policy, this is another issue to think about when making your final decision.

- Don't be afraid to ask questions.

- Ask the staff to explain anything you see and hear that you don't understand. For example, if you hear a person calling out, it may be because they're confused, not because they're being hurt or neglected.

- Ask who to call if you have further questions and write down the name and phone number.

- If a resident or a resident's family wishes, you may talk to them about the care offered at the facility and their experience.

- Don't go into resident rooms or care areas without asking the resident and nursing home staff first. Always knock first and ask a resident before entering their room.

- Residents have a right to privacy and can refuse to allow you to come into their rooms. After your visit, write down any questions you still have about the nursing home or how the nursing home will meet your needs.

Use the "Nursing home checklist" when you visit a nursing home

Take a copy of the "Nursing home checklist" (see pages 26–32) when you visit to ask questions about resident life. Use a new checklist for each nursing home you visit. You can photocopy the checklist or print additional copies at Medicare.gov/nhcompare.

Nursing home checklist

Name of nursing home: _____

Address: _____

Phone number: _____

Date of visit: _____

Is the nursing home Medicare-certified?			
Is the nursing home Medicaid-certified?			
Does the nursing home have the level of care I need?			
Does the nursing home have a bed available?			
Does the nursing home offer specialized services, like a special unit for care for a resident with dementia, ventilator care, or rehabilitation services?			
Is the nursing home located close enough for friends and family to visit?			

Nursing home checklist

Resident appearance	Yes	No	Notes
Are the residents clean, well groomed, and appropriately dressed for the season or time of day?			
Nursing home living spaces	**Yes**	**No**	**Notes**
Is the nursing home free from overwhelming unpleasant odors?			
Does the nursing home appear clean and well kept?			
Is the temperature in the nursing home comfortable for residents?			
Does the nursing home have good lighting?			
Are the noise levels in the dining room and other common areas comfortable?			
Is smoking allowed? If so, is it restricted to certain areas of the nursing home?			
Are the furnishings sturdy, yet comfortable and attractive?			

Nursing home checklist

Staff	Yes	No	Notes
Does the relationship between the staff and residents appear to be warm, polite, and respectful?			
Does the staff wear name tags?			
Does the staff knock on the door before entering a resident's room? Do they refer to residents by name?			
Does the nursing home offer a training and continuing education program for all staff?			
Does the nursing home check to make sure they don't hire staff members who have been found guilty of abuse, neglect or mistreatment of residents; or have a finding of abuse, neglect, or mistreatment of residents in the state nurse aid registry?			
Is there a licensed nursing staff 24 hours a day, including a Registered Nurse (RN) present at least 8 hours per day, 7 days a week?			
Will a team of nurses and Certified Nursing Assistants (CNAs) work with me to meet my needs?			
Do CNAs help plan the care of residents?			
Is there a person on staff that will be assigned to meet my social service needs?			
If I have a medical need, will the staff contact my doctor for me?			
Has there been a turnover in administration staff, such as the administrator or director of nurses, in the past year?			

Nursing home checklist

Residents' rooms	Yes	No	Notes
Can residents have personal belongings and furniture in their rooms?			
Does each resident have storage space (closet and drawers) in his or her room?			
Does each resident have a window in his or her bedroom?			
Do residents have access to a personal phone and television?			
Do residents have a choice of roommates?			
Are there policies and procedures to protect residents' possessions, including lockable cabinets and closets?			

Hallway, stairs, lounges, and bathrooms	Yes	No	Notes
Are exits clearly marked?			
Are there quiet areas where residents can visit with friends and family?			
Does the nursing home have smoke detectors and sprinklers?			
Are all common areas, resident rooms, and doorways designed for wheelchair use?			
Are handrails and grab bars appropriately placed in the hallways and bathrooms?			

Nursing home checklist

Menus & food	Yes	No	Notes
Do residents have a choice of food items at each meal? (Ask if your favorite foods are served.)			
Can the nursing home provide for special dietary needs (like low-salt or no-sugar-added diets)?			
Are nutritious snacks available upon request?			
Does the staff help residents eat and drink at mealtimes if help is needed?			

Activities	Yes	No	Notes
Can residents, including those who are unable to leave their rooms, choose to take part in a variety of activities?			
Do residents have a role in planning or choosing activities that are available?			
Does the nursing home have outdoor areas for resident use? Is the staff available to help residents go outside?			
Does the nursing home have an active volunteer program?			

Nursing home checklist

Safety & care	Yes	No	Notes
Does the nursing home have an emergency evacuation plan and hold regular fire drills (bed-bound residents included)?			
Do residents get preventive care, like a yearly flu shot, to help keep them healthy? Does the facility assist in arranging hearing screenings or vision tests?			
Can residents still see their personal doctors? Does the facility help in arranging transportation for this purpose?			
Does the nursing home have an arrangement with a nearby hospital for emergencies?			
Are care plan meetings held with residents and family members at times that are convenient and flexible whenever possible?			
Has the nursing home corrected all deficiencies (failure to meet one or more state or Federal requirements) on its last state inspection report?			

Steps to choosing a nursing home

Go to a resident council or family council meeting

While you're visiting the nursing home, ask a member of the resident council if you can attend a resident council or family council meeting. These councils are usually organized and managed by the residents or the residents' families to address concerns and improve the quality of care and life for the resident.

If you're able to go to a meeting, ask a council member the following questions and take notes:

- What improvements were made to the quality of life for residents in the last year? _____
- What are the plans for future improvements? _____
- How has the nursing home responded to recommendations for improvement? _____
- Who does the council report to? _____
- How does membership on the council work? _____
- Who sets the agendas for meetings? _____
- How are decisions made (for example, by voting, consensus, or one person makes them)? _____

Visit again

It's a good idea to visit the nursing home a second time. It's best to visit a nursing home on a different day of the week and at a different time of day than your initial visit. Staffing can be different at different times of the day and on weekends.

Notes on second visit: _____

_____

_____

_____

Step 4: Choose the nursing home that meets your needs.

When you have all the information about the nursing homes you're interested in, talk with people who understand your personal and health care needs. This might include your family, friends, doctor, clergy, spiritual advisor, hospital discharge planner, or social worker.

What if more than one nursing home meets my needs?

If you find more than one nursing home you like with a bed available, use the information you got to compare them. Trust your senses. If you don't like what you saw on a visit (for example, if the facility wasn't clean or you weren't comfortable talking with the nursing home staff) you may want to choose another nursing home. If you felt that the residents were treated well, the facility was clean, and the staff was helpful, you might feel better about choosing that nursing home.

What if I'm helping someone make a decision?

If you're helping someone, keep the person you're helping involved in making the decision as much as possible. People who are involved from the beginning are better prepared when they move into a nursing home. If the person you're helping isn't alert or able to communicate well, keep his or her values and preferences in mind.

What if I don't like a nursing home?

If you visit a nursing home that you don't like, look at other options, if available. Quality care is important. If you're in a hospital, talk to the hospital discharge planner or your doctor before you decide not to go to a nursing home that has an available bed. They may be able to help you find a more suitable nursing home or arrange for other care, like short-term home care, until a bed is available at another nursing home you choose. However, you may be responsible for paying the bill for any additional days you stay in the hospital.

33

Steps to choosing a nursing home

Moving can be difficult. However, an extra move may be better for you than choosing to stay at a facility that isn't right for you. Be sure to explain to your doctor or discharge planner why you aren't happy with a facility that they may be recommending.

Once in the nursing home, if you find that you don't like the nursing home you chose, you can move to another facility with an available bed. The nursing home you leave may require that you let them know ahead of time that you're planning to leave. Talk to the nursing home staff about their rules for leaving. If you don't follow the rules for leaving, you may have to pay extra fees.

What information does the nursing home need?

After you choose a nursing home, you will need to make the arrangements for admission. When you contact the nursing home office, it's helpful to have this information ready:

Payment information for nursing home office staff

Insurance information: Provide information about any health care coverage and long-term care insurance you have that pays for nursing home care, health care, or both. This includes the name of the insurance company and the policy number.

Note: If Medicare or Medicaid will cover your nursing home care, the nursing home can't require you to pay a cash deposit. They may ask that you pay your Medicare coinsurance amounts and other charges you would normally have to pay. It's best to pay these charges when they're billed, not in advance. You may have to pay a cash deposit before you're admitted to a nursing home if your care won't be covered by either Medicare or Medicaid.

Information for nursing home staff

- **Information on your medical history:** Your doctor may give the staff some of this information. This includes a list of any current or past health problems, any past surgeries or treatments, any shots you've had, and allergies you have to food or medicine.

- **Information on your current health status:** Your doctor should give the staff this information, including a list of your current health problems, recent diagnostic test results, and information about any activities of daily living that might be difficult for you to do by yourself.

- **A list of your current medicines:** Include the dose, how often you take it, and why you take it.

- **A list of all your health care providers:** Include names, addresses, and phone numbers.

- **A list of family members to call in case of an emergency:** Include names, addresses, and phone numbers.

Health care advance directives

You may be asked if you have a health care advance directive, which is a written document that says how you want medical decisions to be made if you become unable to make decisions for yourself. There are 2 common types of health care advance directives:

1. **A Living Will:** A Living Will is a written legal document that shows what type of treatments you want or don't want in case you can't speak for yourself, like whether you want life support. Usually, this document only comes into effect if you're unconscious.

2. **A durable power of attorney for health care:** A durable power of attorney for health care is a legal document that names someone else to make health care decisions for you. This is helpful if you become unable to make your own decisions.

Steps to choosing a nursing home

If you don't have a health care advance directive and need help preparing one, or you need more information, talk to a social worker, discharge planner, your doctor, or the nursing home staff. You can use the Eldercare Locator to find out if your state has any legal services that help with preparing these forms. See page 7.

Personal needs accounts

You may want to open an account managed by the nursing home, although the nursing home may not require this. You can deposit money into the account for personal use. Check with the nursing home to see how they manage these accounts. You may only have access to the account at certain times. See pages 49–50 for information about your resident rights and protections regarding your money.

Information about Medicare & Medicaid benefits

If you want admission to a nursing home, the nursing home must provide (orally and in writing) and prominently display written information about how to apply for and use Medicare and Medicaid benefits. They must also provide information on how to get refunds for previous payments covered by such benefits.

Section 5:

Paying for nursing home & other health care costs

Nursing home care can be expensive. There are many ways you can pay for nursing home care. For example, you can use your own money, you may be able to get help from your state, or you may use long-term care insurance.

Most people who enter nursing homes begin by paying for their care out of pocket. As you use your resources (like bank accounts and stocks) over a period of time, you may eventually become eligible for Medicaid.

Will Medicare pay for nursing home care?

Medicare generally **doesn't** cover long-term care stays in a nursing home. Even if it doesn't cover nursing home care, you'll need health coverage for hospital care, doctor services, and medical supplies while you're in the nursing home.

Words in blue are defined on pages 53–54.

Medicare covers skilled nursing facility (SNF) care in a Medicare-certified SNF for a limited time after a 3-day qualifying hospital inpatient stay. For more information on Medicare's coverage of SNF care, visit Medicare.gov.

This section explains some of the ways you can pay for a long-term stay in a nursing home, or get help with other health care costs. It includes information about:

- Personal resources (page 38)
- Help from your state (pages 38–40)
- Long-term care insurance (page 41)
- Medicare (pages 41–43)

Personal resources

You can use your personal money and savings to pay for nursing home care. Some insurance companies let you use your life insurance policy to pay for long-term care. Ask your insurance agent how this works.

Important: Be sure to get help before using either of these options. There are important issues you need to understand.

Help from your state (Medicaid)

Medicaid is a joint federal and state program that helps with medical costs for some people with limited income and resources. Most health care costs are covered if you qualify for both Medicare and Medicaid. Most, but not all, nursing homes accept Medicaid payment. Even if you pay out-of-pocket or with long-term care insurance, you eventually may spend down your assets while you're at the nursing home, so it's good to know whether the home will accept Medicaid.

Words in blue are defined on pages 53–54.

Check with the nursing home to see if they accept people with Medicaid. Medicaid programs vary state to state. Most often, eligibility is based on your income and personal resources. Many states have higher Medicaid income limits for nursing home residents. You may be eligible for Medicaid coverage in a nursing home even if you haven't qualified for other Medicaid services in the past.

Sometimes you won't be eligible for Medicaid until you've spent some of your personal resources on health care. Generally, even if you're eligible for Medicaid, all of your income (except for a monthly personal needs allowance) will go to pay your nursing home expenses and Medicaid will cover the rest. To get more information on Medicaid eligibility in your state, call your State Medical Assistance (Medicaid) office. See page 9.

Important things to know about Medicaid

- **Paying for care:** You may have to pay out-of-pocket for nursing home care each month. The nursing home will bill Medicaid for the rest of the amount. How much you owe depends on your income and deductions.

- **Your home:** The state can't put a lien on your home if there's a reasonable chance you'll return home after getting nursing home care or if you have a spouse or dependents living there. This means the state can't take, sell, or hold your property to recover benefits that are correctly paid for nursing home care while you're living in a nursing home in this circumstance.

  In most cases, after a person who gets Medicaid nursing home benefits passes away, the state must try to recover whatever benefits it paid for that person from their estate. However, they can't recover on a lien against the person's home if it's the residence of the person's spouse, brother or sister (who has an equity interest and was residing in the home at least one year prior to the nursing home admission), blind or disabled child, or child under the age of 21 in the family.

- **Your assets:** Most people who are eligible for Medicaid have to reduce their assets first. There are rules about what is and isn't counted as an asset when determining Medicaid eligibility. There are also rules that require states to allow married couples to protect a certain amount of assets and income when one of them is in an institution (like a nursing home) and one isn't.

  A spouse who isn't in an institution may keep half of the couple's joint assets, up to a maximum of $109,560 in 2013, as well as a monthly income allowance. For more information, call your State Medical Assistance (Medicaid) office. See page 9. You can also use the Eldercare Locator to find out if your state has any legal services where you could get more information. You can also get free health insurance counseling from your State Health Insurance Assistance Program (SHIP). See page 9.

- **Transfer your assets:** Most people who are eligible for Medicaid have to reduce their assets first. There are rules about what is and isn't counted as an asset when determining Medicaid eligibility. There are also rules that require states to allow married couples to protect a certain amount of assets and income when one of them is in an institution (like a nursing home) and one isn't.

  Transfers for less than fair market value may subject you to a penalty that Medicaid won't pay for your nursing home care for a period of time. How long the period is depends on the value of the assets you gave away. There are limited exceptions to this, especially if you have a spouse, or a blind or disabled child. Generally, giving away your assets can result in no payment for your nursing home care, sometimes for months or even years.

  Note: Federal law protects spouses of nursing home residents from losing all of their income and assets to pay for nursing home care for their spouse. When one member of a couple enters a nursing home and applies for Medicaid, his or her eligibility is determined under "spousal impoverishment" rules.

  Spousal impoverishment helps make sure that the spouse still at home will have the money needed to pay for living expenses by protecting a certain amount of the couple's resources, as well as at least a portion of the nursing home resident's income, for the use of the spouse who is still at home. For more information about this protection, call your State Medical Assistance (Medicaid) office. See page 9.

  To apply for Medicaid, call your state Medicaid office. They can tell you if you qualify for the Medicaid nursing home benefit or other programs, like Programs of All-inclusive Care for the Elderly (PACE), or home and community-based waiver programs. See page 16.

Long-term care insurance

This type of private insurance policy can help pay for many types of long-term care, including both skilled and nonskilled care. Long-term care insurance can vary widely. Some policies may cover only nursing home care, while others may include coverage for a whole range of services, like adult day care, assisted living, medical equipment, and informal home care.

If you have long-term care insurance, check your policy or call the insurance company to find out if the care you need is covered. If you're shopping for long-term care insurance, find out which types of long-term care services and facilities the different policies cover. Also, check to see if your coverage could be limited because of a pre-existing condition. Make sure you buy from a reliable company that's licensed in your state.

Federal employees, members of the uniformed services, retirees, their spouses, and other qualified relatives may be able to buy long-term care insurance at discounted group rates. For more information about long-term care insurance for federal employees, visit opm.gov/insure/ltc.

Medicare health & prescription drug coverage

Medicare

Medicare is the federal health insurance program for people who are 65 or older, certain younger people with disabilities, and people with End-Stage Renal Disease (permanent kidney failure requiring dialysis or a transplant, sometimes called ESRD).

Paying for nursing home & other health care costs

People can get Medicare **in two ways:**

1. **Original Medicare:** Original Medicare **doesn't** pay for most nursing home care. Most nursing home care helps with activities of daily living like bathing, dressing, and using the bathroom. Medicare covers very limited and medically necessary skilled care or home health care if you need skilled care for an illness or injury and you meet certain conditions.

   For more information on Medicare coverage of skilled nursing facility (SNF) care or home health care, visit Medicare.gov, or call 1-800-MEDICARE (1-800-633-4227). TTY users should call 1-877-486-2048.

2. **Medicare Advantage Plans and other Medicare health plans:** If you belong to a Medicare Advantage Plan (Part C) (like an HMO or PPO) or other Medicare health plan, check with your plan to see if it covers nursing home care. Usually, plans don't help pay for this care unless the nursing home has a contract with the plan. Ask the health plan about nursing home coverage before you make any arrangements. If the nursing home has a contract with your health plan, ask the health plan if they check the home for quality of care.

Medicare prescription drug coverage (Part D)

If you have a Medicare Prescription Drug Plan and live in a nursing home or other institution, you'll get your covered prescriptions from a long-term care pharmacy that works with your plan.
(**Note:** Institutions don't include assisted living or adult living facilities or residential homes, or any kind of nursing home not identified by Medicare.) This long-term care pharmacy usually contracts with (or is owned and operated by) your institution.

Unless someone chooses a Medicare health plan with drug coverage or a stand-alone Medicare drug plan, Medicare automatically enrolls people with both Medicare and full Medicaid coverage living in institutions into Medicare drug plans. If you live in a nursing home and have full Medicaid coverage, you pay nothing for your covered prescriptions after Medicaid has paid for your stay for at least one full calendar month.

If you have Medicare **& live in a nursing home or other institution, you should know:**

- If you move into or move out of a nursing home or other institution, you can switch Medicare drug plans at that time. You can switch Medicare drug plans at any time while you're living in the institution.

- If you aren't able to join on your own, your authorized representative can enroll you in a plan that meets your needs.

- If you're in a skilled nursing facility (SNF) and you're getting Medicare-covered skilled nursing care, your prescriptions generally will be covered by Medicare Part A (Hospital Insurance).

Hospital stays & skilled nursing facility care

If you have Original Medicare or a Medicare health plan, you should know:

- **If you need short-term skilled care in a SNF after an inpatient hospital stay of 3 days or more,** the hospital staff should help you find a Medicare-certified facility that gives the skilled care you need. For more information on Medicare coverage of SNF care, visit Medicare.gov, or call 1-800-MEDICARE (1-800-633-4227). TTY users should call 1-877-486-2048.

- **If you think you're being asked to leave a hospital too soon,** you can ask for a review from a Quality Improvement Organization (QIO). The QIO is an independent reviewer who will give you a second opinion about whether you're ready to leave the hospital. Your hospital services will continue to be paid during the review (except for charges like your coinsurance and deductibles).

- **If you think you're being asked to leave a SNF too soon,** you can ask for a review from your QIO. The QIO, under most circumstances, will give you its decision before Medicare coverage of your skilled nursing care ends.

- **If you're being discharged from a health care setting, like a hospital or SNF:** Use Medicare's "Your Discharge Planning Checklist" to help make sure you have the information you need before you're discharged. To get a copy, visit Medicare.gov.

Words in blue are defined on pages 53–54.

Paying for nursing home & other health care costs

Section 6:
Living in the nursing home

Care plans

The nursing home staff will get your health information and review your health condition to prepare your care plan. You (if you're able), your family (with your permission), or someone acting on your behalf has the right to take part in planning your care with the nursing home staff.

Your care plan is very important. A good care plan can help make sure that you're getting the care you need, help the nursing home understand your personal goals and wishes, and help make your stay better. Your health assessment (a review of your health condition) begins the day you're admitted. A comprehensive assessment must be completed within 14 days of admission. You should expect to get a health assessment at least every 90 days after your first review, and possibly more often if your medical status changes.

The nursing home staff will assess your condition regularly to see if your health status has changed. They will adjust your care plan as needed. Nursing homes are required to submit this information to the federal government. This information is used for quality measures, nursing home payment, and state inspections.

Depending on your needs, your care plan may include:

- What kind of personal or health care services you need

- What type of staff should give you these services

- How often you need the services

- What kind of equipment or supplies you need (like a wheelchair or feeding tube)

- What kind of diet you need (if you need a special one) and your food preferences

- Your health and personal goals

- How your care plan will help you reach your goals

- Information on whether you plan on returning to the community and, if so, a plan to assist you in meeting that goal

Reporting & resolving problems

If you have a problem at the nursing home, talk to the staff involved. For example, if you have a problem with your care, talk to the nurse or Certified Nurse Assistant (CNA). The staff may not know there's a problem unless you tell them. If the problem isn't resolved, ask to talk with the supervisor, social worker, director of nursing, administrator, or your doctor.

Words in blue are defined on pages 53–54.

The Medicare and/or Medicaid-certified nursing home must have a grievance procedure for complaints. If your problem isn't resolved, follow the facility's grievance procedure. You may also want to bring the problem to the resident or family council.

A Medicare and/or Medicaid-certified nursing home must post the name, address, and phone number of state groups, like the State Survey Agency, State Licensure Office, State Ombudsman Program, Protection and Advocacy Network, and the Medicaid Fraud Control Unit. If you feel you need outside help to resolve your problem, call the Long-Term Care Ombudsman or State Survey Agency for your area. See pages 7–10.

Your resident rights & protections

What are my rights in Medicare and/or Medicaid-certified nursing homes?

As a resident in a Medicare and/or Medicaid-certified nursing home, you have certain rights and protections under federal and state law to ensure you get the care and services you need. You have the right to be informed, make your own decisions, and have your personal information kept private.

The nursing home must tell you about these rights and explain them to you in writing in a language you understand. They must also explain in writing how you should act and what you're responsible for while you're in the nursing home. This must be done before or at the time you're admitted, as well as during your stay. You must acknowledge in writing that you got this information.

At a minimum, federal law specifies that nursing homes must protect and promote these rights of each resident:

- **Exercise your right as a citizen of the U.S.:** You have certain rights as a U.S. citizen, including the right to vote.

- **Be treated with respect:** You have the right to be treated with dignity and respect, as well as make your own schedule and participate in the activities you choose. You have the right to decide when you go to bed, rise in the morning, and eat your meals.

- **Participate in activities:** You have the right to participate in an activities program designed to meet your needs and the needs of the other residents.

- **Be free from discrimination:** Nursing homes don't have to accept all applicants, but they must comply with local, state, and federal civil rights laws. If you believe you've been discriminated against, visit hhs.gov/ocr, or call the Department of Health and Human Services, Office for Civil Rights at 1-800-368-1019. TTY users should call 1-800-537-7697.

Living in the nursing home

- **Be free from abuse and neglect:** You have the right to be free from verbal, sexual, physical, and mental abuse, as well as abuse of your money or property (called "misappropriation of property"). Nursing homes can't keep you apart from everyone else against your will. If you feel you've been mistreated (abused) or the nursing home isn't meeting your needs (neglect), report this. You may wish to report abuse or neglect to the nursing home administrator. Depending on your state, the agency that investigates abuse and neglect will be Adult Protective Services and/or the State Survey Agency. See page 10. The nursing home must investigate and report all suspected violations and any injuries of unknown origin within 5 working days of the incident to the proper authorities. The Long-Term Care Ombudsman can also assist by being your advocate and helping you resolve your concerns. See page 7.

- **Be free from restraints:** Nursing homes can't use any physical restraints (like side rails) or chemical restraints (like drugs) to discipline you or for the staff's own convenience.

- **Make complaints:** You have the right to make a complaint to the staff of the nursing home, the State Survey Agency, or the Long-Term Care Ombudsman without fear of being punished. The nursing home must address the issue promptly.

- **Get proper medical care:** You have these rights regarding your medical care:
  - To be fully informed about your total health status in a language you understand.
  - To be fully informed about your medical condition, prescription and over-the-counter drugs, vitamins, and supplements.
  - To be involved in the choice of your doctor.
  - To participate in the decisions that affect your care.
  - To take part in developing your care plan. By law, nursing homes must develop a care plan for each resident. You have the right to take part in this process. Family members can also help with your care plan with your permission.
  - To access all your records and reports, including clinical records (medical records and reports) promptly during weekdays. Your legal guardian has the right to look at all your medical records and make important decisions on your behalf.

— To express any complaints (also called "grievances") you have about your care or treatment.

— To create advance directives (a health care proxy or power of attorney, a living will, or after-death wishes) in accordance with state law.

— To refuse medications or treatment (including experimental).

▪ **Have your representative notified:** The nursing home must notify your doctor and, if known, your legal representative or an interested family member when the following occurs:

— You're injured in an accident and/or need to see a doctor.

— Your physical, mental, or psychosocial status starts to get worse.

— You have a life threatening condition.

— You have medical complications.

— Your treatment needs to change significantly.

— The nursing home decides to transfer or discharge you from the nursing home.

▪ **Get information on services and fees:** You have the right to be told in writing about all nursing home services and fees (those that are charged and not charged to you) before you move into the nursing home and at any time when services and fees change. In addition:

— The nursing home can't require a minimum entrance fee if your care is paid for by Medicare or Medicaid.

— For people seeking admission to the nursing home, the nursing home must tell you (both orally and in writing) and display written information about how to apply for and use Medicare and Medicaid benefits.

— The nursing home must also provide information on how to get a refund if you paid for an item or service, but because of Medicare and Medicaid eligibility rules, it's now considered covered.

Living in the nursing home

- **Manage your money:** You have the right to manage your own money or choose someone you trust to do this for you. In addition:

  — If you deposit your money with the nursing home or ask them to hold or account for your money, you must sign a written statement saying you want them to do this.

  — The nursing home must allow you access to your bank accounts, cash, and other financial records.

  — The nursing home must have a system that ensures full accounting for your funds and can't combine your funds with the nursing home's funds.

  — The nursing home must protect your funds from any loss by providing an acceptable protection, such as buying a surety bond.

  — If a resident with a fund passes away, the nursing home must return the funds with a final accounting to the person or court handling the resident's estate within 30 days.

- **Get proper privacy, property, and living arrangements:** You have these rights:

  — To keep and use your personal belongings and property as long as they don't interfere with the rights, health, or safety of others.

  — To have private visits.

  — To make and get private phone calls.

  — To have privacy in sending and getting mail and email.

  — To have the nursing home protect your property from theft.

  — To share a room with your spouse if you both live in the same nursing home (if you both agree to do so).

  — The nursing home has to notify you before your room or your roommate is changed and should take your preferences into account.

  — To review the nursing home's health and fire safety inspection results.

- **Spend time with visitors:** You have these rights:
  - — To spend private time with visitors.
  - — To have visitors at any time, as long as you wish to see them, and as long as the visit doesn't interfere with the provision of care and privacy rights of other residents.
  - — To see any person who gives you help with your health, social, legal, or other services at any time. This includes your doctor, a representative from the health department, and your Long-Term Care Ombudsman, among others.

- **Get social services:** The nursing home must provide you with any needed social services, including:
  - — Counseling
  - — Help solving problems with other residents
  - — Help in contacting legal and financial professionals
  - — Discharge planning

- **Leave the nursing home:**
  - — **Leaving for visits:** If your health allows, and your doctor agrees, you can spend time away from the nursing home visiting family or friends during the day or overnight, called a "leave of absence." Talk to the nursing home staff a few days ahead of time so the staff has time to prepare your medicines and write your instructions.
  Caution: If your nursing home care is covered by certain health insurance, you may not be able to leave for visits without losing your coverage.
  - — **Moving out:** Living in a nursing home is your choice. You can choose to move to another place. However, the nursing home may have a policy that requires you to tell them before you plan to leave. If you don't, you may have to pay an extra fee.

- **Have protections against involuntary transfer or discharge:** You can't be sent to another nursing home or made to leave the nursing home, unless any of these are true:
    — It's necessary for the welfare, health, or safety of you or others.
    — Your health has improved to the point that nursing home care is no longer necessary.
    — The nursing home hasn't been paid for services you got.
    — The nursing home closes.

  You have these rights:
    — You have the right to appeal a transfer or discharge. If you need help filing an appeal, the Long-Term Care Ombudsman can help. See page 7.
    — The nursing home can't make you leave if you've applied and are waiting to get Medicaid coverage.
    — Except in emergencies, nursing homes must give a 30-day written notice of their plan and reason to discharge or transfer you.
    — The nursing home has to safely transfer or discharge you and give you proper notice of bed-hold and readmission requirements.

- **Form or participate in resident groups:** You have a right to form or participate in a resident group to discuss issues and concerns about the nursing home's policies and operations. Most homes have such groups, often called "resident councils." The home must give you meeting space and must listen to and act upon grievances and recommendations of the group.

- **Have your family and friends involved:** Family and friends can help make sure you get good quality care. They can visit and get to know the staff and the nursing home's rules. Family members and legal guardians may meet with the families of other residents and may participate in family councils, if one exists. With your permission, family members can help with your care plan. If a family member or friend is your legal guardian, he or she has the right to look at all medical records about you and make important decisions on your behalf.

Section 7: **Definitions**

Long-term care: A variety of services that help people with their medical and non-medical needs over a period of time. Long-term care can be provided at home, in the community, or in various types of facilities, including nursing homes and assisted living facilities. Medicare doesn't pay for this type of care if this is the only kind of care you need.

Medicaid: A joint federal and state program that helps with medical costs for some people with limited income and resources. Medicaid programs vary from state to state, but most health care costs are covered if you qualify for both Medicare and Medicaid.

Medicare: The federal health insurance program for people who are 65 or older, certain younger people with disabilities, and people with End-Stage Renal Disease (permanent kidney failure requiring dialysis or a transplant, sometimes called ESRD).

Medicare Advantage Plan (Part C): A type of Medicare health plan offered by a private company that contracts with Medicare to provide you with all your Part A and Part B benefits. Medicare Advantage Plans include Health Maintenance Organizations, Preferred Provider Organizations, Private Fee-for-Service Plans, Special Needs Plans, and Medicare Medical Savings Account Plans. If you're enrolled in a Medicare Advantage Plan, Medicare services are covered through the plan and aren't paid for under Original Medicare. Most Medicare Advantage Plans offer prescription drug coverage.

Medicare health plan: A plan offered by a private company that contracts with Medicare to provide Part A and Part B benefits to people with Medicare who enroll in the plan. Medicare health plans include all Medicare Advantage Plans, Medicare Cost Plans, Demonstration/Pilot Programs, and Programs of All-inclusive Care for the Elderly (PACE).

Definitions

Medicare Prescription Drug Plan (Part D): A stand-alone drug plan that adds prescription drug coverage to Original Medicare, some Medicare Cost Plans, some Medicare Private-Fee-for-Service Plans, and Medicare Medical Savings Account Plans. These plans are offered by insurance companies and other private companies approved by Medicare. Medicare Advantage Plans may also offer prescription drug coverage that follows the same rules as Medicare Prescription Drug Plans.

Original Medicare: Original Medicare is fee-for-service coverage under which the government pays your health care providers directly for your Part A and/or Part B benefits.

Quality Improvement Organization (QIO): A group of practicing doctors and other health care experts paid by the federal government to check and improve the care given to people with Medicare.

Skilled nursing facility (SNF): A nursing facility with the staff and equipment to give skilled nursing care and, in most cases, skilled rehabilitative services and other related health services.

Skilled nursing facility (SNF) care: Skilled nursing care and rehabilitation services provided on a continuous, daily basis, in a skilled nursing facility.

A good nursing home
should function like a
welcoming community
and help you become
and stay involved.

CPSIA information can be obtained at www.ICGtesting.com
Printed in the USA
LVOW10s1449200215

427733LV00013B/353/P